ANALYSIS
of
LAB GIRL

*A FastReads Book Analysis
with Key Takeaways & Review*

TABLE OF CONTENTS

EXECUTIVE SUMMARY 5

EDITORIAL REVIEW... 6

KEY PLAYERS... 7

KEY TAKEAWAYS 8

PART I: Roots and Leaves 8

Key Takeaway: People are like plants: they grow towards the light.
Key Takeaway: Your lab is your home.
Key Takeaway: Writing is a defense against time.
Key Takeaway: Every tree was first a seed that waited.
Key Takeaway: There are two types of people: those who are sick and those who are not sick.
Key Takeaway: The first root to extend, takes the greatest risk.
Key Takeaway: The first real leaf is a new idea.
Key Takeaway: Experiments are not about getting the world to do what you want it to do.
Key Takeaway: Tree rings tell a story of growth, trauma, and perseverance.

PART II: Wood and Knots 13

Key Takeaway: The American South is a mecca for plant growth.
Key Takeaway: Trees & Fungus: Mutually destructive and beneficial.
Key Takeaway: Trees, like businesses, are ruled by a budget.
Key Takeaway: Weeds & Vines are the most resilient.
Key Takeaway: Harsh environments require hardy plants and adaptability.
Key Takeaway: Plants take care of each other.

PART III: Flowers and Fruit... 18

Key Takeaway: Urbanization is stripping the Earth of plant life.
Key Takeaway: A scientist's instruments are a testament to their personality.
Key Takeaway: Trees stand tall in freezing weather.
Key Takeaway: Successful plant sex is rare, but worth it.
Key Takeaway: Plant growth comes at a cost.
Key Takeaway: No sapling's life is perfect, but the parent trees can help.

Key Takeaway: There are many different species of plants in the same plant family.
Key Takeaway: When dealing with plants, it is difficult to tell the end from the beginning.

ABOUT THE AUTHOR **24**

EXECUTIVE SUMMARY

Lab Girl is a thought-provoking analysis of the philosophical similarities between plants and humans and the lessons that science teaches us about life. In a world historically dominated by masculine authority, author Hope Jahren exposes the world of science and professional academia to the reader from the unique perspective of a female scientist. Through her experiences we are introduced to a new way of thinking about the plants all around us, the story they have to tell, and the science that gives these plants a voice. *Lab Girl* is a guide for the young, old, and curious—a story that urges us to seek out our passions and be grateful for the experiences we have along the way, both good and bad.

EDITORIAL REVIEW

Lab Girl hopes to present and analyze the philosophical similarities between plants and humans all through the unique lens of a female scientist. In the end, the arguments are compelling and the analogies effective and insightful, if presented in a terse and obscure way. The organization of the book and the presentations of allegory are at times confusing or disjointed, but this gives the reader a first-person view into the frenzied mind of a scientist. Jahren outlines her experiences, ideas, and behavior as somewhat of a social outcast, which may feel alienating to the reader. However, in this way it is effective at exposing the socially challenging world of academia and professional science, which can be an unwelcoming environment to female scientists.

There is a lot to be learned from plants and from this book, especially in uncovering the sheer diversity of botany and our reliance on the plants that we often ignore. In this way, the book is an effective and compelling philosophical read. Every reader will walk away with a different lesson from *Lab Girl*, which is the goal of the book.

KEY PLAYERS

Hope Jahren: Main protagonist and first-person narrator. She is a quirky female geobiologist who has an affinity for plants and Chesapeake Retrievers.

Bill: Bill Hagopian is a laboratory manager and close professional partner to Jahren. They met while Jahren was working as a grad student at Berkeley. Bill is known for his rough-edged demeanor, good sense of humor, and patient affinity for helping others.

Jahren's Mother: Hope's mother is a tough, resourceful, if relatively detached figure in this text. Their relationship is strained. Hope's memories of her mother are most strongly tied to their shared garden and how adept her mother was at keeping things growing.

Jahren's Father: Hope's father is a community college professor in Minnesota. He is also an emotionally distant but hard working figure in this text. The Swedish background of Hope's family is often blamed for the lack of emotional equity.

Clint Conrad: Hope's husband and geophysicist. They met at a barbecue in 2001 while Hope was living in Baltimore. Clint is a patient, stable character and the first love of Jahren's life. He is described as a sweet, solid, and loving character.

KEY TAKEAWAYS

PART I: ROOTS AND LEAVES

Key Takeaway: People are like plants: they grow towards the light.

The author's childhood is highlighted in detail to offer some historical perspective and explain to the reader how the author became the person she is today: a scientist. Jahren grew up in Minnesota—a harsh environment with long, brutally cold winters and short, but lush, growing seasons. Her Scandinavian family is portrayed as an emotionally distant clan who often go days without speaking to one another. Because of this, the author grows up wary of those who openly offer affection, emotion, and personal information. Instead, the author takes solace in two distinct environments: her mothers' garden and her fathers' laboratory.

In the garden, she learns about efficiency and productivity as her pragmatic mother works within the short growing season to grow large amounts of only the most resilient crops that can be frequently harvested and stored throughout the winter. In the laboratory with her father, Jahren thrives on the curiosity, persistence, and purpose required to perform scientifically sound experiments. Given this background, it is no wonder that Jahren grows up to be a geobiologist: a plant scientist. The author's evolution highlights the notion that people will pursue what makes them thrive.

Key Takeaway: Your lab is your home.

For Jahren, the laboratory is not a singular room, but a sanctuary of her own design. Many connections are drawn in the description of Jahren's lab, but one key theme is that everyone has a lab. The lab is a place of complete comfort. It is one's home.

Connections are drawn between a lab and one's own personal introspective headspace. This is a protected place where you are free to flex your creativity and operate untethered to constraints of the outside world. You decide who to let into your lab.

"The door is locked and I know everyone who has the key. Because the outside world cannot come into the lab, the lab has become the place where I can be the real me" (pg. 19).

The lab is also compared to a church and religion as a whole, where one knows the routine and rituals involved in daily operation. It is a sacred place that is never closed and always accepting.

"On holidays, when the rest of the world is closed, my lab is open" (pg. 19).

Key Takeaway: Writing is a defense against time.

Science teaches us that writing everything down in detail is essential to meaningful results. Jahren applies this practice to her life, explaining that writing is the key to remembering the past. She uses the example of her favorite spruce tree near her childhood home, citing in detail the commonalities between the growth of a tree and the growth of a human. This tree was special to her and by writing down her memories, feelings, and perception of this tree, she is immortalizing the spruce and her memory of it.

Key Takeaway: Every tree was first a seed that waited.

Seedlings are used as a symbolism for growth and perseverance against all odds. Seeds can wait for hundreds or even thousands of years to start growth and many seeds never grow into the plants they came from. In the wild, seeds will wait for the opportune combination of circumstances for which to grow into trees.

"In the right place, under the right conditions, you can finally stretch out into what you are supposed to be" (pg. 31).

This anecdote is used to describe the conditions and difficulties involved with personal growth. We are all given one chance to be who we should be but growth takes patience and perseverance.

Key Takeaway: There are two types of people: those who are sick and those who are not sick.

The author details her time working in the pharmacy department of a hospital while attending college. This job required her to fill and transfer bags of mixed medications to ill patients, a duty which she initially believes to be highly important. Her outlook quickly sours, aided by the drone of monotony and the depression of sickness and death around her. At first, she perceives the hospital as a place of sterile control and hope, but as she spends more time there she finds a workplace that is constantly behind, heavily understaffed, and chock full of inefficiency, bureaucracy, and waste. Disenchanted, she sees the job of medicine as a ferrying of people from sickness to death. She identifies that there are two types of people in the world: those who are sick and those who are not sick. The people who are not sick, she muses, should get to work helping those people that are sick.

While she respects the people who work to save the lives of others, the job is not for her and she quickly leaves for a job at a research laboratory.

Key Takeaway: The first root to extend, takes the greatest risk.

Once settled in the earth, the first thing to emerge from a seed is the root. This breakout is associated with a myriad of risks, dangers, and hopeful gambles for which the plant is risking its life. If successful, this first root becomes the taproot—the main anchor and lifeline for the mature plant. From there, many ancillary roots spring from the base of the plant forming an interconnected web of plant life.

Jahren draws similarities between the risk, necessity, and even fate associated with the first root to the academic plunge into her Ph.D. While attending Berkeley, she serves as a graduate student assistant instructor on a number of academic experiments in the heart of California's Central Valley. During this time, she meets a boy named Bill to whom she is immediately drawn because of his quirky nature and obvious intellect. She is intrigued by the mystery of his past and over time develops a fondness for him. She eventually approaches her advisor to recommend Bill for a job in the lab, who agrees and offers the job to Bill on the condition that he is Jahren's responsibility.

For readers, this section is about taking risks to pursue your passions and that sometimes the most terrifying life choices are the most rewarding. Drawing connections back to the plant, your passion and potential vocation become the taproot for which you nurse joy and reward out of life.

Key Takeaway: The first real leaf is a new idea.

When a plant begins its ascent skyward from the grounded seed, the first leaf to grow is a brand new idea for the organism. There is a vague genetic blueprint for how the plant should grow and how to build a leaf, but every leaf is unique and the potential for improvisation is huge. Obviously, this analogy is akin to the unique personalities, ideas, and career paths for each human being. There are many different kinds of plants, but even plants of the exact same genus and species are individually unique; they are products of their environment.

Some of these first leafs turn out to be the first improvisations of their kind and can lead to widespread evolution throughout an entire species. Jahren uses the example of the first cholla cactus choosing to turn its first leaf into a spine to maximize dew condensation and reduce shade on the stem of the plant. This adaptation allowed the cactus to flourish in the climate it is in today.

In this example, we see how some groundbreaking ideas can alter the growth of a plant, a human, or even a society in enormous ways.

Key Takeaway: Experiments are not about getting the world to do what you want it to do.

This is a lesson that the author learns the hard way while conducting her first funded experiment in Colorado. The experiment requires her to examine the flowering patterns of a grove of trees, but after spending the summer in the area, the trees never end up flowering.

Jahren is devastated by this perceived failure and she initially falls into a panicked depression. However, she eventually comes to the realization that instead of focusing on what the trees WEREN'T doing, she should have been focusing on what they WERE doing. What was causing these trees to forego flowering? What were they doing instead?

In this analogy, experiments and experiences are interchangeable. Oftentimes, we cannot change the situations we find ourselves in but if we focus on what we cannot change, we will never learn anything. Instead of focusing on what is NOT happening, we can focus on the situation itself and what we can learn from it. We may not be able to control certain experiences, but we can learn and grow from them regardless.

Key Takeaway: Tree rings tell a story of growth, trauma, and perseverance.

The rings on a tree can tell a lot about the quality of its life. Larger rings indicate periods of abundant resources and quick growth, while slimmer rings indicate periods of stress. Oblong rings can indicate the falling of a branch and the compensation of nutrients to make up for the weight shift. All trees have rings that are both thin and thick and all of these rings tell one unified story that parallels the story of many a human life: perseverance.

After receiving her Ph.D., Jahren lands an assistant professor position in Atlanta. This is a period of stress and transition for the author as she again transitions from the comfort of her academic home in Berkeley to a professional teaching career on the other side of the country. As a professor, she struggles through stress, anxiety, and lack of sleep, all of which take a toll on her. She invites Bill out to join her as a paid lab assistant and they are excited to set-up their very first personal lab. However, upon his arrival they are discouraged to find that the underfunded and abandoned lab on campus is in poor shape.

If we were going to compare this time period in Jahren's life to the rings on a tree, this time would be marked with a very thin traumatic ring indeed. But just like the tree, she does the only thing she can do; she perseveres.

Everyone, no matter how gifted or impoverished, experiences hard times and good times. This yin-yang cycle is a shared experience that humans and plants have in common. The important thing is to continue growing and persevering through the thin rings so we can experience the thick rings.

PART II: WOOD AND KNOTS

Key Takeaway: The American South is a mecca for plant growth.

The environment and seasonal temperatures of the American South make for optimal growing conditions for almost any type of plant. Warm, humid summers and relatively mild winters allow plants to thrive and grow in abundance. Jahren compares this plant growth to the economic boom in Atlanta between 1990 and 2000, during which many Fortune 500 companies flocked to the city.

It is during this time that Jahren and Bill are experiencing significant growth of their own, both personally, academically, and spiritually. The duo is working tirelessly to put together their first lab, running on a minimal budget and pinching pennies at every turn, sacrificing their personal comforts for the success and development of the lab. Although they both face a large looming debt and they are financially strapped, this is a time of happiness and freedom for the both of them as they work to develop a lab of their own.

Key Takeaway: Trees & Fungus: Mutually destructive and beneficial.

Fungus is often portrayed as the mechanism for organic decay, which it absolutely is. However, fungus can also create a mutually beneficial relationship with trees that allow both parties to maximize water uptake, maintain ground stability, and encourage growth in hostile environments. Either of these organisms can survive on their own but for some reason they join forces to assist in each other's growth.

Jahren uses this metaphor to explain her relationship with her trusty employed research assistant, Bill. These two people are dissimilar in almost every way, except for one: they share a mutual love for science. Their personalities are totally complimentary, with one person's strength filling in for the others' weakness. This is further explained by the dichotomy of their researching styles. Jahren identifies as a "Lumper," choosing to lump research details together into a larger picture. Bill is a "Splitter" because he separates the details of his work into neat categories. Although these two personality types will inevitably clash, both are necessary for thorough and accurate scientific work.

Long lasting and effective partnerships rely on complimentary personalities. Too many similarities in a partnership may lead to inadequate decision making or "Group Think" in which similar opinions band together and neglect the opinions of others. No matter the differences, each partner must bring something unique to the table to enable growth, just like the fungus and the trees.

Key Takeaway: Trees, like businesses, are ruled by a budget.

Each year during the growing season, trees must allocate the right amount of resources in the right way to survive. Leaves must be organized in such a way that maximizes exposure to sunlight. The chlorophyll in the leaves that allows for photosynthesis is built on minerals which the trees must mine from the soil. In order to mine those minerals, the tree must absorb and evaporate 8,000 gallons of water per year. These are a few of the many factors that need to be considered, measured, and executed by the tree to maintain growth.

"When building foliage, a tree must budget for each leaf individually and allocate for each position relative to the other leaves" (pg.120).

Much like the tree, the life of an academic scientist is dictated by the funding and budget that they receive. The type of research that Jahren does is known as "curiosity driven research" meaning that the goal of the research is not profits from a product. The only funding available for this type of research comes from the National Science Foundation (NSF) which doles out $7.3 billion every three years, $6 million of which is allocated for paleobiologists like Jahren. Divided amongst all paleobiologists in the nation, each scientist is receiving roughly $165,000 for 3 years of research. From there, cuts are distributed to the sponsoring University, lab employees like Bill, and taxes, leaving only about $10,000 for 3 years of equipment, lab work, supplies, and travel.

Key Takeaway: Weeds & Vines are the most resilient.

Vines & weeds are some of the most virulent, hardy, and ambitious plants in the botanical kingdom. They madly compete for resources in the form of water, sunlight, space, or scaffolding, often clinging madly to any solid structure in their vicinity.

"A vine becomes whatever it needs to be and does whatever it must in order to make real its fabulous pretensions" (pg. 126).

These plants are opportunists, requiring a disturbance such as the plowing of agriculture or the digging of industry to survive. Oftentimes these disturbances are man-made and although humans may openly besmirch their existence, we are creating a world in which they can thrive.

"We don't resent the audacity of the weed...we resent its fantastic success" (pg. 127).

Jahren implies that there are similarities between weeds and the early academic life of herself and Bill. As young quirky professionals, this is a time when they are both trying to make a name for themselves. They are working long hours, competing against their more seasoned colleagues, and fighting to hit deadlines and budgets. Money is scarce for Jahren, but more so for Bill, who proves to be the more resilient "weed" of the two, electing to split his living quarters between the laboratory and a small van to make due on his meager salary. Despite their tenuous living situation and challenging work environment, both Jahren and Bill rarely complain.

Some of the strongest and most resilient people are the vines and weeds of society. They take what resources they can get their hands on and make the most of them, keeping their eye on the goal: growth at any cost.

Key Takeaway: Harsh environments require hardy plants and adaptability.

The desert is among one of the harshest growing environments on planet Earth. Combine the brutal temperature swings with the lack of resources and you have a climate in which only the most resilient plants survive.

"The desert is like a lousy neighborhood: nobody living there can afford to move" (pg. 142).

There are a handful of cactus species that will go entirely dormant for extended periods of time, pulling up their roots and draining their chlorophyll. Seemingly dead, these plants can resurrect within 24 hours when the climate swings in their favor.

During her tenure as a professor in Atlanta, Jahren battles with psychological bipolar swings between periods of manic highs and paralyzingly depressive lows. During one of these manic swings, she ambitiously organizes a trip for her team and any willing students to a conference in San Francisco, despite not having the funds to book airfare. In the frenzied state, she patches together a route, rents a school-owned van, and decides to make the trip cross-country in less than a week in the middle of winter. Ignoring advice from friends and colleagues, she drives straight into a storm and ends up flipping and crashing the van into a ditch, endangering herself, all of her students, and Bill.

Throughout this brush with death and her psychological mood swings, Bill stays by her side the entire time, seemingly unfazed. Jahren is inspired by this unbroken loyalty and realizes how lucky she is to have a partner like him.

In this analogy, Bill is the most like the cactus, sticking with Jahren through even the most tumultuous times. Throughout these stories, Bill remains the constant pillar of strength for Jahren, no matter how tough times get. He always seems to resurrect himself when the conditions call for it. These types of relationships are very important and should be valued.

Key Takeaway: Plants take care of each other.

The Sitka willow tree in Sitka, Alaska is the focus of a study in which the trees were found to be talking to and defending each other against insect invasion. When a grove of willows comes under attack from an invasive caterpillar, the trees in the grove began to secrete chemical insecticide to ward off the bugs. The trees also release an airborne chemical pheromone to warn other trees in the area of the danger. Those pheromones are picked up by willows miles away from the initial attack, who began to secrete the insecticide themselves. In this way, it can be argued that the trees are taking care of one another.

Using this analogy, Jahren again exposes her admiration and appreciation for her lab partner Bill. Jahren continues to fight with her psychological swings and anxiety into the spring of 1999. She is constantly worried about achieving her personal success as a scientist as well as the drastic implications of failure for both herself and Bill. Much like the Sitka Willow, Bill senses her worry and inserts himself as the voice of reason, logic, and lighthearted care. He urges her to seek medical help with her anxiety and not to worry about his personal salary, as he will stick with her through it all.

Throughout this section, special emphasis has been placed on the value of loyalty. We can tell that loyalty is something that Jahren values very highly and she espouses the benefits of having people in your life who show you loyalty.

"Because I know the transcendent value of loyalty, I've been to places that a person can't get to any other way" (pg. 174).

PART III:
FLOWERS AND FRUIT

Key Takeaway: Urbanization is stripping the Earth of plant life.

Billions of years ago, the Earth began as a barren grey wasteland of rock. Slowly but surely plant and animal life crawled out of the ocean and spread on land, creating the green continents that we know today. Urbanization is the only process capable of systematically turning the Earth back into the grey rock that it once was, a process that is accelerating every year.

"*The amount of urban area in the United States is expected to double in the next 40 years, displacing a total area of protected forest the size of Pennsylvania*" (pg. 177).

In 1999 Jahren uproots her life in Atlanta with Bill and moves their entire laboratory to John Hopkins in Baltimore, supposedly the most tree-impoverished state in the domestic US.

Key Takeaway: A scientist's instruments are a testament to their personality.

Many instruments a scientist needs cannot be purchased over the counter or online. Oftentimes, to achieve the results that the scientist is looking for, these instruments need to be heavily modified, tweaked, or custom built from the ground-up. Once these instruments are built and tested, the scientist can then share those findings and his process with the community. Such is the process of innovation in the world of scientific instruments.

These machines, however, can become quirky and unique to the scientist that built them. Jahren and Bill are given the opportunity to adopt a collection of scientific instruments from an old mentor. They ponder over a particularly large mass spectrometer machine, littered with patch-welds, taped fixes, and scribbled tips and notations written in permanent ink. Just by analyzing the outside of the machine we can learn a lot about the unique personality of the scientist who built it and why.

"There is a singular fascination to be indulged when we stop and stare at the piecework of a previous scientists' hands, amazed over the care taken with the peripheral elements, just as we are dazzled by the hundred tiny brushstrokes that magically agglomerate into one small boat on the horizon within a pointillistic painting" (pg. 86).

Key Takeaway: Trees stand tall in freezing weather.

Winter in the arctic latitudes means 6 months of freezing weather with little to no light. Such drastic weather makes it impossible for many forms of life to thrive, but trees do so by carefully adapting to their environment. When they sense the lack of sunlight which signals a coming winter, they begin the process of hardening their cell walls, turning the watery sap into a thick viscous fluid that can't be frozen. Sunlight becomes the biological clock that they rely on for survival.

"These plants know that when your world is changing rapidly, it is important to have identified the one thing that you can always count on" (pg. 193).

This allegory on frozen trees precedes the story of Jahren and Bill's trip to the frozen tundra of Northern Canada. This barren landscape was once lush with conifer forests but is now a frozen desert. They are trying to understand why the once thriving, frozen forest has retreated from this area. During this trip, she and Bill are within close proximity to each other day after day for weeks on end. Instead of becoming exhausted with one another's presence, they become more relaxed and comfortable.

Again, the reader is brought back to the theme of loyalty and reliability. This valued partnership is serving as an example of what true friendship really means.

Key Takeaway: Successful plant sex is rare, but worth it.

Plants successfully breed when one plants' pollen is fertilized in the flower of a neighboring plant. This seems like an easy enough task at the outset, but because plants are immobile and fertilization requires touch, the task becomes a little more difficult. There are many factors required to make this transfer successful such as insects, wind, or weather. More often, plants self-fertilize, meaning that no new genes are added to the gene pool. For the species to persist, there must be some real fertilization that takes place.

This analogy precedes the story of how Jahren met her husband, Clint, and it highlights the desperation and social struggles of a scientist like Jahren in the dating pool. This is a scientist who was essentially married to her work for the first half of her career, more comfortable in the lab than going on dates. Many people she tried to date were exhausted with the constant barrage of plant conversation and couldn't handle the long hours she spent away from home in the lab. It makes sense then, that Clint is a scientist himself and is familiar with the lifestyle.

"The love that I have to give someone had been packed too tightly and too long in a small box, and so it all tumbled out when opened" (pg. 206).

Key Takeaway: Plant growth comes at a cost.

A flowering plants' growth follows a measurable and predictable trajectory. Although these growth patterns may be different from one species to another, the one constant is that during reproduction, the plant shrinks as nutrients and resources are redirected to the flowering and seeding process. The reproduction process takes a measurable toll on the plant, sacrificing a bit of itself to perpetuate the species.

Jahren uses this analogy to outline her particularly difficult pregnancy and the physical, emotional, and psychological toll that it enacted on her body. For years she depended on medication to treat her psychological issues but during the earlier stages of pregnancy, the standard operating procedure is for women to immediately cease this medication—a practice which helps the baby but may have devastating effects on the mother's mental health. For weeks, Jahren lapses back into the symptoms for which she was being treated, experiencing drastic mood swings.

Once back on the medication, her mental state begins to level out, but she is barred from doing the one thing that helps her maintain sanity: lab work. This is a brutal blow to her morale and her respect for her employer suffers.

Jahren eventually gives birth to a healthy baby boy with whom she is obsessed in every way. Her pregnancy has obviously taken a toll on her, much like the plants, but the end result makes it all worth it.

"Perhaps it will be one of the great privileges of my life to watch him grow and give him what he needs, and let him take my love for granted" (pg. 229).

Key Takeaway: No sapling's life is perfect, but the parent trees can help.

When a seed falls to Earth and takes root in the soil beneath its parent, these saplings are forever in their parents' shadow. This is potentially a disadvantage, as it limits the sunlight that can reach the sapling. However, the parent tree does help with water uptake, transferring water from its own roots to those of the sapling so that the small plant can continue to grow and perpetuate the species.

"No parent can make life perfect for its offspring, but we are all moved to provide for them as best we can" (pg. 231).

In 2006, Jahren learns that Bill's father has passed away while she is working at a laboratory and living with her family in Norway. She is heartbroken and paralyzed between her desire to comfort Bill and not having the words to make that comfort possible. Instead, she organizes a research trip for both of them to Ireland and they set off on a familiar journey of scientific exploration and directionless meandering. On this trip, she sees just how affected Bill is from his fathers' passing and she does the only thing she knows how to do: she distracts him with science.

They spend this trip gathering hundreds of samples for an experiment. This work seems to take Bill's mind off of his father but when they reach the airport, their hard-earned samples are confiscated and thrown away by the airport gate agent. Jahren is devastated and embarrassed, but Bill plays the role of optimist, explaining how much research they got done and planning a new trip to gather new samples.

Although Jahren does not consider herself to be a parental figure to Bill, it is clear that she loves him and has an internal desire to care for him and his feelings. This trip, although not perfect, demonstrates Jahren's willingness to care for Bill. This is also a turning point for Bill, who has never necessarily played the role of optimist, progressing through the mourning process.

Key Takeaway: There are many different species of plants in the same plant family.

The *Arecaceae* family encompasses thousands of different palm tree species, all of which are distinct in their own way. Each palm is suited for the environment that they live in.

Human families are much the same. Although a family of four may reside in the same house and share the same lineage, each person in the family is different in their own way. Jahren comes to learn how wonderfully different her son is from her and how unique each of their upbringings has been. The love and affection that Jahren yearned for as a child is now being bestowed on her son, as if she is making up for the shortcomings of her own upbringing.

"Every kiss that I give my child heals one that I had ached for but was not given – indeed, it has turned out to be the only thing that ever could" (pg. 256).

Key Takeaway: When dealing with plants, it is difficult to tell the end from the beginning.

This principle is applicable in many forms. Roots, once severed from the stem that they sprouted, can live underground for years. Standing tree trunks will continue to sprout new growth even after being cut down. In this way, tree life is hard to stamp out.

"In the end, trees die because being alive has simply become too expensive for them" (pg. 268).

In this final section, Jahren reflects on the times that she and Bill have spent together in the lab and the lessons they learned. She finds that her minor contributions to science are just a part of a constantly evolving and growing cultural understanding, the goal of which is to make the world a better place for our children.

"Together we are building something that will fill our grandchildren's grandchildren with awe, and while building we consult daily the crude instructions provided by our grandfathers' grandfather" (pg. 278).

In the end, Jahren finds acceptance and solace in the fact that she does not have all the answers and never will. As a woman, she has faced many obstacles in the male-dominated realm of science. She says that her success comes from her ability to listen and oftentimes ignore the advice and judgements of her colleagues.

"I have accepted that I don't know all the things that I ought to know, but I do know the things that I need to know" (pg. 277).

ABOUT THE AUTHOR

Hope Jahren is an American Geobiologist, writer, mother, and wife. She currently resides in Oslo Norway where she runs the Jahren Laboratory researching stable isotope biogeochemistry at the University of Oslo. She works hand-in-hand with her lifelong professional partner Bill Hagopian

THE END

If you enjoyed this analysis, please leave an honest review on Amazon.com…it'd mean a lot to us!

If you haven't already, we encourage you to purchase a copy of the original book.

Made in the USA
Middletown, DE
13 December 2021

55684326R00015